Gifted and Black

Written by

Rev. Dr. Edonna Alexandria

Gifted and Black—Get a jump on life. Your color is a Gift!

Copyrights© 2014 by Umayat Spiritual Education Circle for Self- Realization Publishing Company

All rights reserved. No part of this book may be used or reproduced in any manner whatsoever without the written and signed permission of the author, except in the case of brief quotations embodied in critical articles or review.

13 ISBN: 978-0-9785663-7-1

www.giftedandblack.info

Printed in the United States of America

Dedicated to my daughters, Nayo and Kai Alexandria-Jones, with love.

This Book Belongs to:_____

Why did God make me Black? My friends at school said God left me in the oven too long. Why do my friends call me tar baby, as if it is a curse word? What did I do wrong for this curse of Blackness? These are the thoughts I have sometimes because I am often teased for my dark skin.

Do you ever think it's hard to be yourself? It's difficult to be dark-skinned. Still, in my own eyes, I'm pretty great.

My name is Tara. I'm telling my story because no child should go through life sad and alone. My mother told me writing would help me feel better. As a matter of fact, I want it to help someone else. So here's my story.

I live in a place where you won't catch anybody walking alone at night. I live in Los Angeles, in the Willowbrook section, better known as Watts.

I'm always scared in this place. My body shivers in fear every time I hear people curse and fight. I wish I had headphones so I could drown them out. I hate hearing nonsense 24/7. My breaking point is when I hear gunshots and see the policemen chase people through our neighborhood in cars or helicopters.

I just go to school. After school, I am cooped up in my house for the rest of the day.

I love and hate school. I love it because it's what I am good at. I keep my head in the books and my nose out of other people's business. I am a straight-A student, and everyone knows it. I don't mean to be a ham or anything, however that's the truth. What I hate about school is other students tease me. They tease me for my smartness and my skin color.

It's recess and my friends Tasha, Natiya and I were playing double Dutch together. The ropes hit the ground and turn in a circular motion as my feet jump through the ropes. We're all that. You can hear us sing:

Teddy Bear, Teddy Bear turn around!
Teddy Bear, Teddy Bear touch the ground!
Teddy Bear, Teddy Bear shine your shoe!
Teddy Bear, Teddy Bear skidoo!

My friends and I are minding our own business when Vincent and Tyrone showed up. My heart starts to race, but I try to ignore them. Vincent says, "Hey Tyrone, man, have you ever seen something so Black and smart like little butt Tara? Ha-ha!"

His words cut so deep, I want to stop jumping and punch him in the face. However, mama said, sticks and stones can break your bones, moreover words never hurt. I am sorry to say, but words do hurt.

Tyrone bursts out laughing like a hyena. "No, man. I don't think you can get any BLACKER than that," he exclaims. "Even the frying pan would run from her because she is so Black. She could scare midnight! Ha-ha!"

I am burning with rage. I know I should turn the other cheek like my mother always says I should, but I've had enough! I stop jumping, cross my arms and yell, "You know what? Y'all just jealous. You all so dumb, you can't even spell "rum". Yo' daddy drink so much, he can't find his way home for tripping on his bottom lip!"

Tasha, Natiya and I start laughing our heads off. Tasha says, "That's a good one!" Tyrone turned red in the face, but I don't realize he is coming at me. Before I know it, he pushes me on the ground and hits me in the mouth.

Tyrone hits me so hard I start to see red stars. When I lift myself from the ground, I almost fall back down but Natiya and Tasha catch me. I am so dizzy. It takes me a while until my balance is straight. I go to the principal's office and tell them what happened. Five minutes later...

Tyrone is in the principal's office. He doesn't protest and accepts his two-day suspension. He was wrong and if he couldn't take the heat, he should have stayed out of the kitchen! My head finally stops hurting and my lip isn't bleeding. My heart still hurts because it isn't the first time I've been teased for being Black and smart.

As soon as I get home I tell my mama everything. I talk so much I don't realize we have company. It is Ms. Williams, my mother's social worker. I am surprised she is here.

She's nice. I consider her my guardian angel. She pulls out her mirror and says, "Come here child. Look into the mirror and tell me what you see."

"Tara," I replied.

"I am looking at a beautiful little Black girl who is going places," Ms. Williams says. I smile because those words started to close some of my wounds. "When the next person calls you black, just say, "The blacker the berry, the sweeter the juice," she says.
I laugh my head off, but she is serious.

"Giftedness and blackness are not shameful. The world doesn't reward anybody for cuteness or dumbness, and ignorance comes in all shades. So don't worry about those no good boys, chasing after you, because they don't mean you any good. You can have brains, education, common sense and still be beautiful."

"Preach!" my mama shouts. "Honey, I was fine as wine, and always had some pretty-boy hanging on my arm or kissing my neck. Nevertheless, look at me now. I tried following up with those boys, but they just left me miserable. The only good thing they gave me was you. Moreover since you were born, I've been on welfare and living in the ghetto still trying to get my G.E.D after all these years," she says.

Ms. Williams gives me a big hug. "Honey, at one time the whole world was filled with nothing BUT black people who were so smart. Even today, people can't figure out how they built things," she says. "They built the pyramids, ships to explore distant lands and drew solar systems in the sky because of what they saw with their inner third eyes, not with telescopes. They even created the game of double Dutch you like so much."

Ms. Williams continued her tales of our great history: "There was a time when all the world knew of black folk without equal. The earth was filled with our wisdom and the glory of African people."

"A time of great black queens and kings using scribes to tell our story,"

"On pyramids and tombs in stone, so they can't deny our glory."

"And being Black as the night was no cause for fright because the wisdom we taught made our spirits so bright!"

"We built pyramids and ships to explore in far-off lands, drew charts from the stars to record the life and times of all of man. We called ourselves "Kem- ites" which meant blackest of all men – to remind us all forever that dark skin is no sin!"

Then Ms. Williams makes me stand in the mirror and say these words:

"I'm beautiful.
I'm bold. I'm smart. I'm strong.
I'm powerful."

Nothing in this world is going to knock me down, because I'm gifted and I'm Black. And like my ancestors the Kem-ites I am super proud of that fact!

From then on, I vow to say those exact words every morning and night. I go into my room and sit at my desk and begin to write in my journal. I spill my whole heart out. I cry. I am more confident than before. My self-esteem soars and it feels like I am floating with the clouds in the sky.

I begin to write what is on my heart and my mind. I want to remember being gifted and Black is no curse but, above all, a blessing. I even wrote a double Dutch song about it. Wanna hear it? Here it goes:

Pyramid, Pyramid what's your story, Pyramid, Pyramid you're my glory, Pyramid, Pyramid I built you, Pyramid forever my dark skin too!

Author's Epilogue

Finally, I am proud of my color and intelligence. People would call me names. I would roll my eyes and turn the other cheek and nobody could break me. I had a strong ego and placed myself on a pedestal like all the kings and queens. I have pride and self- worth, yet I never forgot where I came from. Yes, I am from the ghetto. Despite this, it didn't tear down my future or stop me from achieving my goals. I accepted the things I couldn't change and worked on what I could. I made up my mind to leave the ghetto by going to college. I had dreams and I was going places. After telling my stories in college and becoming the best speaker at my university, I began making big moves.

Appendix:
Double Dutch First Lady Style

A. Getting in the Double Dutch Ropes

1. Gather 3–8 people needed to play the game;

2. Choose two people to turn the ropes and one to jump in;

3. Left arms turn the rope clockwise while right arms turn counterclockwise from the elbow. Hold rope with thumb and forefinger. Curl the rest of your fingers under your thumb;

4. Jump through the ropes when the rope closest to you hits the ground, (for instance, if you are on the right hand side of the turner, you jump in when the rope in their left hand hits the ground.) then move to the center of the rope;

5. Find your rhythm. Turn ropes high and at the required speed for the double Dutch rhyme or music;

6. Once jumping, try moving back and forth along the rope, turning around jumping with one foot or adding other jumpers;

7. Sing the special songs the rope turners sing while the jumpers jump in rhythm. (Some examples of rhymes are given at end of this book. Or why not make your own!);

8. As a street game, you make up the rules of who goes first and of how many games you have to jump to win. When playing in competition, you follow the rules of "the game" just as you would in any other competition that awards trophies and prizes.

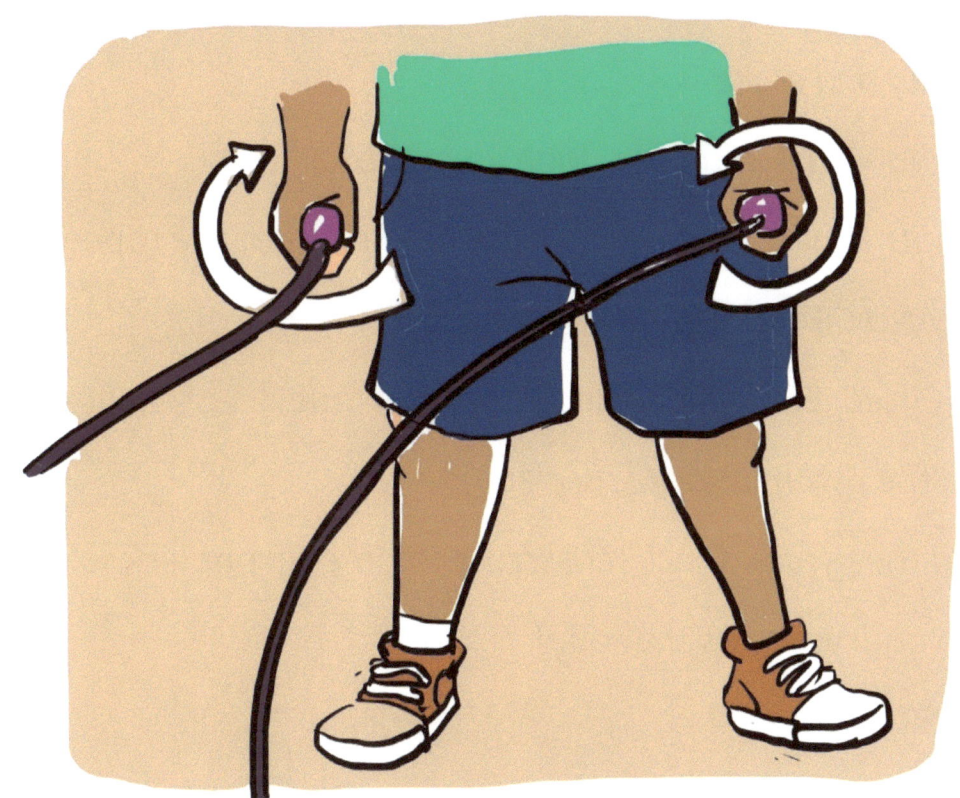

B. The Turners

1. The turners should stand with legs in a wide straddle or shoulder-width apart. The hands should turn small circles to maintain speed and control

over the rope. Wrists should be kept still with a tight fist around the rope. Turners must be in rhythm with the jumper by listening to and watching the jumper's feet.

C. Playful Double Dutch Rhymes

Enjoy these double Dutch rhymes when practicing your new or developing skill.

1. "BLACK QUEEN"

Black Queen, Black Queen, create your world, Now lets see you do the twirl

1, 2, 3, 4, 5, 6…

Full of beauty and grace

Let me see you jump and pace [High knees up]

Now let another queen take your place [Jump out of the ropes]

2. "BLACK AND GIFTED, BLACK AND GIFTED"

Black and Gifted, Black and Gifted [Jump X 4 times]

All around the pyramid rock [Turn 360]

Can you do the pyramid rock [crisscross 10 times; front kick 10 times]

[Fast jump until you miss the rope]

3. "DR. THOMAS"

In 1975, Dr. Thomas earned a medical degree from Johns Hopkins University School of Medicine. She went on to an orthopedic residency at Yale, where she was the first female orthopedic resident. Later she became the first black female orthopedic doctor.

Dr. Thomas fixed one arm. [Put one hand behind back]

Dr. Thomas fixed the other arm. [Put the other hand behind back]

Dr. Thomas fixed one shoulder. [Put one shoulder up]

Dr. Thomas fixed the other shoulder. [Put the other should up]

Dr. Thomas fixed one leg. [Jump on one leg]

Dr. Thomas fixed the other leg. [Jump out of the ropes]

D. Competitive Double Dutch

1. Competition teams will consist of three members; only one member may be a male. This is called a Singles team.

2. A Doubles team is made up of four members, only two members may be male. All athletes in grades 3-8 must compete on their same grade level. In the high school division, athletes in grades 9, 10, 11, and 12 may be mixed.

E. Entering The Ropes

1. Jumpers must be able to enter and exit the ropes. They exit the ropes on the opposite side they came into the ropes.

F. Compulsory Test

Note: Testing for both Singles and Doubles teams consists of five tricks which must be performed in the following order.

1. Two right turns on the right foot towards the right direction;

2. Two left turns on the left foot towards the left direction. (Jumpers should do the turns on the count of 8 to complete the turns, and they must end up facing the same direction they started, see picture above);

3. Two crisscross jumps: right foot over left;

4. Two crisscross jumps: left foot over right.

G. High Steps

1. Ten high steps: alternating jumps counting only the left foot with the jumper's knee being lifted waist high and the thigh parallel to the floor (See picture above);

Tip: When the jumper makes a mistake in Compulsory, the jumper should start from where they made the mistake and continue. Skills should not be repeated.

H. Speed Test

1. This is a test where the jumper jumps the rope using alternating footwork for 2 minutes.

2. An official will count jumps on the left foot only.

Tip: The jumping motion for Double Dutch speed comes from the waist down. The upper body remains motionless and a good jumping posture involves the feet close together and the waist bent slightly forward.

Tip: The position should be comfortable for the jumper but the upper body should remain still.

Tip: Excess movement wastes energy, thus causing the jumper to tire easily.

I. Violations in Speed And Compulsory Testing

Mistake (-10.0)

Drop Rope (-10.0)

Poor Sportsmanship/Bad Attitude (-15.0)

Bad Entry or Exit (-5.0)

Jewelry/Hair Accessories (-15.0)

Sloppy Uniform [i.e.; shirt hanging out] (-15.0)

Coaches: Please practice with your students before a competition at least three days a week.

Contact Page

For more information on gaining jumping and coaching skills, double Dutch fundraising and contest or voicing your opinion on color prejudice, visit our website at www.giftedandblack.info

Youtube channel:
https://www.youtube.com/channel/UCHipdkUjrD_qGvrQ3sutdqw

Twitter: https://twitter.com/DrEdonnaA

Scan our QR code with your smart phone or visit our web-site for additional information and products at: www.giftedandblack.info

Thank you for purchasing our book, we hope you have double loads of fun using it and building your self-esteem!

About The Author

Dr. Edonna is not limited to any conventional or narrow methods of teaching. She has spent the past 21 years studying alternative techniques of educating and empowering youth. Her unique style allows her to harness the power of creative storytelling lessons combined with yoga and Double Dutch. Dr. Edonna's experience as a Health and Physical Education teacher provided fertile ground to put her expertise to work in some of the most challenging schools in America. Her complementary talents enable her to transform chaotic, violent P.E. classes into organized fitness classes. All with the single purpose of inspiring, and empowering students by teaching them invaluable lessons in anti-bullying, fitness, and ethnic pride. She conducts training workshops for Health and P.E. Teachers and regular teachers on Health and Fitness and Anti-Bullying. Additionally, Dr. Edonna conducts parent and student assemblies. Contact her to set up a visit at your school.

www.ingramcontent.com/pod-product-compliance
Lightning Source LLC
Chambersburg PA
CBHW042004150426
43194CB00002B/125